Nelson/Word Multi-Media Group And Systems Media Present

The Andy Griffith Show
Bible Study Series
Volume 1

Participant's Guide

Study Notes Written By
Joey Fann
Drew Maddux
Amy Morland
Stephen Skelton

The Andy Griffith Show Bible Study Series, Volume 1
Published by Nelson Word Multi-Media Group
A division of Thomas Nelson Publishers

Copyright © 2000 by Systems Media

Printed in the United States of America
ISBN 0-8499-8816-0

For Information
Call Thomas Nelson Publishers 1-800-251-4000
www.thomasnelson.com

Foreword

When you mention a Bible Study based on The Andy Griffith Show most people immediately become curious. You can almost hear their minds turning and see the sparkle in their eyes. "Of course", they say. "In today's society, we can learn a lot from the citizens of Mayberry." And when you think about it, the concept becomes obvious. Lessons dealing with the way we treat each other and how to appreciate the small blessings in life immediately come to mind. But when you look a little closer, you begin to discover something deeper: Timeless morals and values that we hold dear are presented in a way that we can readily understand.

To some, using a secular television show as a theme for an informal Bible study may seem like a novel approach. But the message behind the lessons is not new at all. As you will see, the focus of this study is not the episode itself, but the values it demonstrates. These observations allow us to look into our own lives and discuss how we might handle similar situations today. But we don't stop there. We also look to the Scriptures to seek God's guidance as we face these daily challenges of life.

When Brad Grasham and I began teaching lessons based on Mayberry, we had a common goal. We wanted to share with others what we already knew: Mayberry isn't about a place, it's about a lifestyle. It's about loving your neighbor as yourself. It's about training up a child in the way he should go. It's about helping each other through trying times. And when we are able to incorporate these lessons into our lives today, maybe Mayberry isn't as far away as we think.

Joey Fann

About the Authors

Joey Fann is a co-instructor of the Back to Mayberry concept, the basis for *The Andy Griffith Show* Bible Study Series. He pioneered the creation of a weekly Bible class using *The Andy Griffith Show* on his website at barneyfife.com. Fann lives in Huntsville, Alabama with his wife Nicole.

Drew Maddux is president and founder of Systems Media, LLC, a multi-media content company committed to providing entertainment for edification. By joining media and ministry, the company seeks to impact Christians in their everyday lives. Maddux lives in Nashville, Tennessee with his wife Tara.

Amy Morland is director of creative affairs for Systems Media. Her television credentials include writing for ABC, CBS, and WB networks as well as producing for TNN. Morland lives in Nashville, Tennessee with her husband Jeff and three children.

Stephen Skelton is director of development for Systems Media. His background includes producing for Dick Clark Productions and writing for *America's Dumbest Criminals*. He is a member of *The Andy Griffith Show* Rerun Watchers Club. Skelton lives in Nashville, Tennessee with his wife Ashlee and daughter.

About Our Host

Dennis Swanberg is a well-known motivational speaker, teacher, preacher, counselor and comedian. Dr. Swanberg also sketched the charicatures of Mayberry folk included in this study. His nationally broadcast television show, *Swan's Place*, is aired to over one million households. He has authored two books: *Is Your Love Tank Full?* and *Swan's Soup & Salad for Saints & Sinners*. Dr. Swanberg lives in West Monroe, Louisiana with his wife Lauree and their sons, Dusty and Chad.

Table of Contents

The Andy Griffith Show
Bible Study Series
Volume 1-Session 1

"Rafe Hollister Sings"

Session One
"Rafe Hollister Sings"

The notes for "Rafe Hollister Sings" deals with some serious issues regarding how we treat one another. In this study, we will look at prejudice and at how easy it can be to judge someone. We'll also discuss peer pressure and how to have the courage to do the right thing. Finally, we will consider how we can incorporate an attitude of unconditional acceptance in our own lives.

Session Overview

BIBLICAL PRINCIPLE
A Parable from Mayberry

PERSONAL REFLECTION
Finding the Barney Within

INDIVIDUAL APPLICATION
What Would Andy Do?

ACTION POINTS
Building a Better Barney

Scriptures cited in the video include:

1. **James 1:17a** Every good gift and every perfect gift is from above. NKJV
2. **Matthew 7:1** "Judge not, that you be not judged. NKJV
3. **1 Samuel 16:7c** Man looks at the outward appearance, but the LORD looks at the heart. NKJV
4. **James 2:13b** Mercy triumphs over judgment. NKJV
5. **Ephes. 4:1b-2** Walk worthy of the calling with which you were called, with all lowliness and gentleness, with longsuffering, bearing with one another in love. NKJV

Judging Others

MATTHEW 7:1-5

"Judge not, that you be not judged. For with what judgment you judge, you will be judged; and with the measure you use, it will be measured back to you. And why do you look at the speck in your brother's eye, but do not consider the plank in your own eye? Or how can you say to your brother, 'Let me remove the speck from your eye;' and look, a plank is in your own eye? Hypocrite! First remove the plank from your own eye, and then you will see clearly to remove the speck from your brother's eye."

In this passage, Jesus warns against hypocritical judgment. That does not mean that critical thinking is wrong, but God wants us to be *discerning* instead of *condemning* (see Mt 7:15-20). We are to judge others as we want God to judge us.

"Well what's wrong is that Rafe don't have no trained singing voice that's what's wrong."

"You want to get up there with the rest of us and make a fool out of yourself, Rafe?"

BIBLICAL PRINCIPLE
A Parable from Mayberry

Take a few moments to think about how each of the following reacted to the idea of Rafe singing at the Musicale. Describe their reaction in one or two words:

Andy	Thought his singing was great
Barney	was jealous
Rafe Hollister	Rafe didn't want to at first
Music Director John Masters	thought he had the "Perfect voice"
Opie	thought he sounded good
Mayor Stoner	Didn't want him to
Mrs. Jeffries	Didn't want him to
Martha Hollister	loved it
League president, Mrs. Dennis	loved it
Musicale audience	loved it

Privately, which character most closely matches your own initial reaction? In what way?

Rafe, I'd be surprised

"That don't mean you have to stop singing, Rafe. You just go ahead and do it. You sing in the bathtub, don't you?"

"Well, you go right ahead and do that..."

Rafe:
"Well, I reckon since they ain't never around when I'm taking a bath, I best go on over there."

Some folks had strong opinions about Rafe that kept them from seeing his musical gift.

What was Barney's biggest concern in the beginning of the episode? Who do you think he looking out for?

_____

_____

_____

Why do you think Barney failed to appreciate Rafe's beautiful voice?

_____

_____

Barney explains the finer points of singing to Rafe.

What was the mayor and Mrs. Jeffries true concern in opposing Rafe?

_____

_____

_____

Why do you suppose Andy tried to change Rafe's appearance? Was that really in Rafe's best interest?

_____

_____

_____

How did Rafe respond to other people's negative behavior toward him?

_____

_____

_____

PERSONAL REFLECTION
Finding the Barney Within

✝ Ᵽɾᵢₙcᵢₚₗₑ: **How _____ judge others, God will judge _____.**

The characters in Mayberry often comically exaggerate thoughts and feelings that we all share to some degree. If we are honest, we, too, prejudge others because of physical appearance, level of education, perceived financial status, and even color of skin. We also tend to magnify others' faults while minimizing our own, especially the faults we share with them (see Ro 2:1). Jesus teaches us to redirect our focus.

Were you surprised that Rafe had such a beautiful voice? If so, why?

_____

_____

_____

How did you feel about the way that the mayor and Mrs. Jeffries tried to control Andy and Rafe?

_____

_____

_____

Would you want the mayor and Mrs. Jeffries as your closest friends? Why or why not?

_____

_____

_____

Rafe Hollister?!! Represent Mayberry?

Mrs. Jeffries: "Rafe Hollister simply is not presentable... and to present him at my organization, a club that has been dedicated to the finer things? Never!"

"Rafe's already been told he won."

Mayor Stoner: "Rafe Hollister was your idea. You just march yourself right out to his place and tell him he will not be needed!"

"Boy, I'm in trouble. If he shows up at the Musicale looking like that, Mayor and Mrs. Jeffries will have a fit!"

"I guess we'll have to go out and get him some clothes."

It is very evident that some of the Mayberry folks are self-*centered* rather than self-*aware*. In the thick of the above discussion, did you find yourself sharing their faults? If so, it is easy to do—especially in the midst of peer pressure!

✝ Principle: **We should examine _____ before we criticize _____.**

(Do you feel like you've just been tricked?)
Yes ☐ No ☐

Seeing Rafe and Martha's joy, Andy just can't swing the axe.

PERSONAL APPLICATION
What Would Andy Do?

Andy at times stumbles along, but he learns from his mistakes. Trying to make everyone happy can sometimes keep us from doing the right thing, as we saw in this episode. God is more concerned that we *love* others, rather than *please* them.

MATTHEW 22:37-40
Jesus said to him, 'You shall love the LORD your God with all your heart, with all your soul, and with all your mind.' This is the first and great commandment. And the second is like it: 'You shall love your neighbor as yourself.' On these two commandments hang all the Law and the Prophets.

Most of us find it hard not to give in to pressure to act like others around us, rather than following the law of love. Consider the following examples.

Faced with potential rejection, would you tend to be defensive like Barney or uncompromised like Rafe? Explain.

_____

_____

_____

Rafe prepares to sing (provided he can breathe).

How does Rafe's behavior demonstrate the law of love?

_____

_____

_____

Under the pressure of public opinion, do you bend like Andy or resist like the music director John Masters?

_____

_____

_____

How does John Masters demonstrate the law of love? Is he active or passive?

_____

_____

_____

Given social pressure, would you tend to be snobbish like Mrs. Jeffries or loyal like Martha?

_____

_____

_____

Have you ever abandoned a friend in an embarrassing situation?

_____

_____

_____

✝ Principle: **God calls us to love _____ as we love**

_____.

John Masters:
"So genuine. A fully natural feeling. A perfect pitch. Yes."

"Amazing he's kept it to himself all this time."

"Mayberry is going to have a representative we can all be proud of at the Musicale."

Mrs. Dennis:
"And what a perfectly marvelous idea, having him dressed that way. It made the selection so much more authentic."

"Mr. Hollister, will you favor us with another selection?"

Can others truly know us based only on our appearance? No. Are we guilty of some faults we readily find in others? Of course! Nevertheless, our common goal as Christians is to accept others with the same kind of compassion we want for ourselves—unconditional kindness, forgiveness and, most importantly, love.

Colossians 3:12-14
Therefore, as the elect of God, holy and beloved, put on tender mercies, kindness, humility, meekness, longsuffering; bearing with one another, and forgiving one another, if anyone has a complaint against another; even as Christ forgave you, so you also must do. But above all these things put on love, which is the bond of perfection.

✞ Principle: **We should make _____ our aim in relating to _____.**

Consider the following action points and plan to do at least one of them this week, with God's help.

I will resist prejudice by:
❑ Talking to someone I previously would have avoided because of their attitude, dress or race.
❑ Asking God to reveal my own faults when I am critical of someone else.

I will resist negative peer pressure by:
❑ Refusing to play favorites among my friends.
❑ Defending a person others are disparaging.
❑ Resisting the popular thing when it is not the right thing.

I will practice acceptance of others by:
❑ Serving someone I consider "less important" than myself.
❑ Offering help to a stranger in need.
❑ Showing kindness to someone who has hurt me.

The mayor and Mrs. Jeffries can hardly believe their ears.

NOTES

NOTES

The Andy Griffith Show
Bible Study Series
Volume 1-Session 2

"Opie and the Spoiled Kid"

Session Two
"Opie and the Spoiled Kid"

The notes for "Opie and the Spoiled Kid" will focus on the reasons why we work. We will explore the value of a strong work ethic and the proper use of money. We will also discuss the need for parents actively to teach their children values in these two important areas of life. Always a joy, Andy and Opie's father/son conversations here are classic.

Session Overview

BIBLICAL PRINCIPLE
A Parable from Mayberry

PERSONAL REFLECTION
Finding Your Inner Opie

INDIVIDUAL APPLICATION
What Would Andy Do?

ACTION POINTS
With an Opie-like Trust

Scriptures cited in this video include:

1. **Genesis 2:15** Then the LORD God took the man and put him in the garden of Eden to tend and keep it. (NKJV)
2. **Galatians 6:7** Do not be deceived, God is not mocked; for whatever a man sows, that he will also reap. (NKJV)
3. **1 Timothy 6:18** Let them do good, that they be rich in good works, ready to give, willing to share. (NKJV)
4. **Proverbs 3:12** The LORD disciplines those he loves, as a father the son he delights in. (NKJV)
5. **Proverbs 13:11** Wealth gained by dishonesty will be diminished, But he who gathers by labor will increase. (NKJV)

The Value of Work

MATTHEW 25:14-18

Matthew 25:14-18

"For the kingdom of heaven is like a man traveling to a far country, who called his own servants and delivered his goods to them. And to one he gave five talents, to another two, and to another one, to each according to his own ability; and immediately he went on a journey. Then he who had received the five talents went and traded with them, and made another five talents. And likewise he who had received two gained two more also. But he who had received one went and dug in the ground, and hid his lord's money." (NKJV)

From this parable, we discern that God wants us to work. Idle people squander the resources He supplies them (see 2 Thes. 3:11-13). As He gives us opportunities to use our gifts, we work for God—not for man—no matter what our job.

BIBLICAL PRINCIPLE
A Parable from Mayberry

Arnold made quite a splash when he hit the Mayberry scene. He had some "interesting" ideas about what should be required of kids and his behavior challenged the accepted norm in a number of ways. In one or two words, describe the reaction of each of the following as they meet (or "see") Arnold for the first time.

Lady leaving the grocery store	
Opie	
Barney	
Andy	
Mr. Winkler (at beginning)	
Mr. Winkler (at end)	

Privately, which character most closely matches your own initial reaction?

_____

How would meaningful work help Arnold?

_____

_____

_____

_____

(Admiring Arnold's new Intercontinental Flyer)

"Seventy dollars? Gosh, you must've been saving up for it since you was a kid!"

Arnold:
"My dad bought it for me."

Arnold:
"A quarter? For a job like this?"

"Oh, no. Besides this, I take out the ashes, keep the wood box filled, and set the table every night."

Arnold:
"Oh boy! Did your old man see you a-comin'."

Opie and Arnold had very different views of work and the need to contribute to society.

Why do you think Opie worked without complaining?

_____

_____

_____

_____

How did Arnold's attitude toward work reflect other aspects of his character?

_____

_____

_____

_____

Mr. Winkler wanted to provide well for his son, as do all parents. However, he overlooked some important gifts that would make Arnold truly happy. What were they?

_____

_____

_____

_____

Opie made a mistake when he trusted Arnold's opinion about money over Andy's guidance. Which viewpoint prevailed in the end? Why?

_____

_____

_____

Opie does some serious listening to the "worldly" Arnold.

Arnold meets Andy—head on!

PROVERBS 22:6
Train up a child in the way he should go,
And when he is old he will not depart from it.

✝ Principle: **Our ability and opportunity to _____ are _____ from God.**

Like Opie, we sometimes lose sight of who we really work for and why. Ultimately, Opie worked to obey and please his father. He loved his *father*, not necessarily the work.

Would you say that currently you are working for your heavenly Father? Why or why not?

_____

_____

_____

_____

Does that mean that working for money is wrong? No. Money is necessary to support ourselves (2 Thes. 3:10), share with others (1 Tim. 6:18) and to give back to God (Mal. 3:10). Money only becomes a problem when it is our primary goal. The pursuit of power, control, and independence through money and possessions ends in death (Mt. 16:25-27). Furthermore, materialism never satisfies us, because God made humans with a thirst for things eternal (Ecc. 3:11).

Without his parent's guidance, Arnold developed a materialistic value system. Do you sometimes think that a lot of money would make you happy? Why or why not?

_____

_____

_____

_____

Arnold:
"They owe it to you. You're not supposed to work for your allowance. What do you think allowance means?"

"I don't know."

Arnold:
"It means money the kid is allowed to have."

✠ Principle: **To _____ money is godly; the _____ of money corrupts us.**

As with many things in our lives, our parents mainly teach us our work ethic and attitudes toward money. Teachers, employers, and others who are important to us also contribute to our growth.

Andy, Mr. Winkler, and Barney each had different philosophies about how to teach children their values. Andy took an active approach to instill his values for work in Opie. Mr. Winkler was passive and taught Arnold mainly by his actions—for good or for bad. Barney theorized that he would motivate his "phantom child" through fear of punishment.

How would you describe the way your parents (role models) taught you values about work and money?
❑ Active guidance
❑ Passive model
❑ Fear of punishment
❑ Other

Opie gives Arnold's advice a shot.

Do you think your present attitude toward work and money is godly? Why or why not?

_____

_____

_____

_____

We should honor our parents for giving us what they could (De 5:16). Nevertheless, some of us received inadequate training in the important areas of work and money as children. Does that mean we are stuck for good? No. It only means our Heavenly Father will need to fill the gap now as adults (Pro. 19:20). And *He* is very good at it.

1 TIMOTHY 6:18
Let them do good, that they be rich in good works, ready to give, willing to share,

Our work is not a separate entity from the rest of our life. Andy and Mr. Winkler worked to provide for their families. Our work and the money we earn bless those we love.

How can your work and income directly bless others? (Employers, co-workers, family, society)

_____

_____

_____

On the other hand, if we work mainly to *impress* or *indulge* others, we will never satisfy them or ourselves.

How often would you say that you give your loved ones "things" in an effort to make them happy?
❑ Frequently
❑ Occasionally
❑ Rarely
❑ Never
Which do you think is optimum? _____

We all, at times are tempted to "keep up with the Joneses". What would you tell someone who asked you why that was wrong?

_____

_____

_____

Arnold steps over the line, en route to the woodshed.

"Well, as you get bigger, why you'll be doing more and more work for more and more return and that good feeling will get bigger. Do you understand what I mean?"

"Yeah. The bigger you get, the tireder you get."

" Is Arnie gonna get spanked, Pa?"

"Don't you think he deserves it"

"I don't wanna say. After all, he is one of my own kind."

MATTHEW 6:19

"Do not lay up for yourselves treasures on earth, where moth and rust destroy and where thieves break in and steal; but lay up for yourselves treasures in heaven, where neither moth nor rust destroys and where thieves do not break in and steal."

Our possessions will not be with us in heaven—only *people*. To work best in the world, we should have a heavenly focus. We can win and serve others through our actions and our attitudes toward God's gift of work.

Consider the following action points and plan to do at least one of them this week, with God's help.

I can bless my employer by:

- ❑ Thanking God for His gift of work and His provisions.
- ❑ Asking God to show me how to grow in my attitudes toward work and money, and seeking His grace to change.
- ❑ Telling my boss I appreciate how hard he works to support his employees.
- ❑ Making sure I do not abuse my break and lunch schedules.

I can bless my loved ones by:

- ❑ Refusing to work unnecessary overtime.
- ❑ Planning and *doing* a weeknight activity with them.
- ❑ Surprising them with a small gift just to show my love (especially if such a gift is rare).

I can pass on my work ethic by:

- ❑ Sharing with a friend or family member the good things my parents taught me about work and how that has helped me as an adult.
- ❑ Developing an age-appropriate chore list and allowance for each child in my family.
- ❑ Showing patience with people learning new tasks at work or home and tactfully offering tips to help them succeed.

NOTES

NOTES

The Andy Griffith Show
Bible Study Series
Volume 1-Session 3

"The Rivals"

Session Three
"The Rivals"

The notes for "The Rivals" will focus on the basics of Christian mentoring. We will highlight its value in every stage of life. We will also spotlight the danger of wrong motives and the effectiveness of just listening to another's story. While parents play the most important role in mentoring their children, we will explore how others can also play a significant part. And, of course, the episode would not be complete without Barney's romantic maneuverings in pursuit of *l'amour toujours amour*.

Session Overview

BIBLICAL PRINCIPLE
A Parable from Mayberry

PERSONAL REFLECTION
Ousting the Barney Inside

INDIVIDUAL APPLICATION
What Would Andy Do?

ACTION POINTS
Empathy Like Thelma Lou's

Scriptures cited in this video include:

1. **Isaiah 64:8b**: We are the clay, and You our potter; And all we are the work of Your hand. (NKJV)
2. **Psalm 127:1**: Unless the LORD builds the house, They labor in vain who build it. (NKJV)
3. **Hebrews 5:2**: He can have compassion on those who are ignorant and going astray, since he himself is also subject to weakness. (NKJV)
4. **Psalm 33:11**: The counsel of the LORD stands forever, The plans of His heart to all generations. (NKJV)
5. **Psalm 32:8**: I will instruct you and teach you in the way you should go; I will guide you with My eye. (NKJV)

Serving as Mentors

PROVERBS 19:20

Listen to counsel and receive instruction,
That you may be wise in your latter days. (NKJV)

In the proverb above, Solomon points out the importance of mentoring to gain wisdom. Our own perspective is limited and ideally, we should seek many mentors during the course of our lives (see Pr. 15:22). When we obtain wisdom, Solomon asserts that we gain long life, wealth, honor, and peace (Pr 3:16-17).

The process should not stop there, however. We pass on the wisdom we gain to others, as we then become the mentors. This is especially true in raising up the next generation.

BIBLICAL PRINCIPLE
A Parable from Mayberry

Opie has his first stirrings of love for a cute little girl named Karen. His efforts to get Karen to also like him eventually involves three others as well: Andy, Thelma Lou, and Barney. Describe in one or two words how each of the following reacted to Opie's new and challenging feelings.

Karen Burgess	
Andy	
Barney	
Thelma Lou	
Opie	

Who proved to be helpful? How?

_____

_____

_____

Opie gives Karen the grand tour.

"See that door back there? Well, that's the door I go through when I empty out the trash baskets. Of course, emptying trash is only part of it. Most of the time, we're busy hunting down desperate criminals."

"What's on today, Pa? Any roadblocks or stakeouts or three-eights or four-twos?"

When Opie had a question or a problem, he turned to his dad. He wasn't too timid—or proud—to ask for help. Opie was willing to admit he did not have all the answers.

What makes Opie easy to mentor?

_____

_____

_____

How did Andy make Opie comfortable to come to him for help?

_____

_____

_____

Andy and Opie relax as they discuss marriage—and kids.

Why do you think Andy did not give detailed instructions to Opie regarding his behavior with Karen? What would you say was Opie's greatest need?

_____

_____

Why did Opie follow Barney's advice about winning girls? Did Barney's advice help Opie grow?

_____

_____

_____

Judging from the final scene with Karen and Opie, do you think someone was mentoring Karen, as well? Why or why not?

_____

_____

_____

PHILIPPIANS 2:3-4
Let nothing be done through selfish ambition or conceit, but in lowliness of mind let each esteem others better than himself. Let each of you look out not only for his own interests, but also for the interests of others. (NKJV)

✝ Principle: **We should put _____ needs _____ our own.**

Barney is always putting his foot in his mouth because it is very difficult for him to see things from another person's viewpoint. Unfortunately, Barney's weakness does not impact just himself. It also affects the person that he is trying to help, because Barney's self-focus colors his advice and renders it useless.

Would you say that you sometimes give others advice out of your own needs or weakness? Why or why not?

_____

_____

_____

As Christian mentors, we must weigh our opinions as carefully as we would our actions. A simple "I don't know" is appropriate when we don't!

Have you ever found yourself giving someone advice before you listened carefully to the problem? If so, what was the outcome?

_____

_____

_____

Opie does his best to sweep Karen off her feet.

Thelma Lou:
"He sure is lovesick, isn't he?"

"Yeah. I suspect your fudge brownies might just provide the antidote, though."

"Waiting for your girl? You know, I got an idea for you. This time, when she comes by, you step right out and you say to her, 'Well, here I am you lucky girl! If you play your cards right, maybe I'll let you walk with me!'"

Karen watches as Opie goes off hand-in-hand with Thelma Lou.

When "the girl" Opie impressed turned out to be Thelma Lou, Barney was very upset. When we advise others based on what serves ourselves, we injure both them and ourselves.

If Barney's motive was to help Opie, how would you expect him to respond to Opie's success? What was Barney's actual motive?

_____

_____

_____

Why is it important for a mentor to have pure motives?

_____

_____

_____

Do you agree that every mentor should also seek to be mentored? Why or why not?

_____

_____

_____

At each new stage in our lives, we can learn a great deal from others who have gone before us (Pr. 1:5, 19:20). Likewise, we can teach those who follow. God calls us to be an interdependent people (Jas. 5:13-20).

Do you have any mentors? If not, do you think it might be a good thing to pray for?

_____

_____

_____

ROMANS 12:15-17

Rejoice with those who rejoice, and weep with those who weep. Be of the same mind toward one another. Do not set your mind on high things, but associate with the humble. Do not be wise in your own opinion. Repay no one evil for evil. Have regard for good things in the sight of all men. (NKJV)

Mentoring is really another word for love. A good mentor tries to place herself in another's situation. Thelma Lou did not give Opie any advice. She had never been a young boy experiencing the stress of trying to get a girl's attention. But she did know how it felt to be unsure of oneself in a new situation. She simply tried to help Opie get his mind off his "problem" and feel good about *himself*. Her mentoring was different than Andy's, but also important for Opie's growth.

Karen waits to see Opie outside the sheriff's office.

If Opie had come to you dejected, how could you respond to him? (Consider actions as well as words)

_____

_____

_____

_____

Do you know a child in your neighborhood, a friend, or a co-worker who simply needs someone to affirm them?

❑ Yes
❑ No

Have you ever considered being that person?

❑ Yes
❑ No

"Now, you know I like Opie. I always have. He's well-mannered, he's obedient, well brought up. He's a good little fella..."

"Well, I'm glad to hear that."

"But lately, he's getting to be nothing but a pest!"

"I hardly think of Karen anymore, now that Thelma Lou's my girl."

"So Thelma Lou's your girl, huh?"

"Uh-huh. And guess what? Today's Saturday, so I get to spend the whole day with her!"

ACTION POINTS
Empathy Like Thelma Lou

1 THESALONIANS 5:14-15

Now we exhort you, brethren, warn those who are unruly, comfort the fainthearted, uphold the weak, be patient with all. See that no one renders evil for evil to anyone, but always pursue what is good both for yourselves and for all. (NKJV)

Warn, comfort, uphold, be patient, pursue the good for ourselves and for all. Paul is not charging us each to engage in heavy counseling. Mentoring—and being mentored—is within the reach of us all. It is humble giving and receiving.

✟ Principle: **We should actively seek ways to _____ wisdom and _____ it with others.**

Consider the following action points and plan to do at least one of them this week, with God's help

I will increase my awareness of other's needs by:
❑ Asking God to show me others as He sees them.
❑ Keeping my head up and *looking* at others as I go about my day.

I will determine my strengths by:
❑ Asking God and others who know me well to tell me what they see as my strengths.
❑ Allowing God to place me in circumstances where I recognize a need I can meet.
❑ Joining or starting a group where I can both teach and be taught (e.g., a bible study, parenting group, church sports team).

I will recognize my shortcomings by:
❑ Asking God to show me where I need to grow. Asking someone I trust.
❑ Seeking a friend, church member, or class to teach me a skill that I don't have, but could use to help others.

"Hey Barn, can you answer the phone. You're closer."

34

NOTES

The Andy Griffith Show
Bible Study Series
Volume 1-Session 4

"Aunt Bee's Medicine Man"

Session Four
"Aunt Bee's Medicine Man"

The notes for "Aunt Bee's Medicine Man" will study the nature of deception—how we are deceived, why we are deceived, and how we can help free someone else from their deception. Also in this episode, watch Aunt Bee find the fountain of youth in an elixir with a funny taste.

Session Overview

BIBLICAL PRINCIPLE
A Parable from Mayberry

PERSONAL REFLECTION
Resisting the Aunt Bee Within

INDIVIDUAL APPLICATION
What Would Andy Do?

ACTION POINTS
Overcoming Darkness with Light

Scriptures cited in this video include:

1. **Proverbs 4:23** Keep your heart with all diligence, For out of it spring the issues of life. (NKJV)
2. **Proverbs 14:15** The simple believes every word, But the prudent considers well his steps. (NKJV)
3. **Proverbs 10:23** To do evil is like sport to a fool, But a man of understanding has wisdom. (NKJV)
4. **Proverbs 10:9** He who walks with integrity walks securely, But he who perverts his ways will become known. (NKJV)
5. **Philippians 1:9a** And this I pray, that your love may abound still more and more in knowledge and all discernment. (NKJV)

The Power of Deception

1 PETER 5:8
Be sober, be vigilant; because your adversary the devil walks about like a roaring lion, seeking whom he may devour.
(NKJV)

Peter speaks from experience. Though he was a man of strong faith, he was also subject to deception at critical moments (cf. Mt. 16:21-23; 26:69-75). When situations in life cause us to question, we must be careful where we search for answers. During those times, we are most vulnerable to deceivers, who tell us what we want to hear and promise what we think we need.

BIBLICAL PRINCIPLE
A Parable from Mayberry

Colonel Harvey was a bald-faced liar who preyed on the innocent. His false charm and manipulation through flattery were transparent to some, but others believed him. Briefly describe the reaction of each character below when they first meet the Colonel.

Aunt Bee	Thought he was great
Barney	He was nut
Andy	didn't like him
Opie	Thought he was a con man
Colonel Harvey	loved himself
Townspeople	interested
Ladies Aide	They couldn't tell

Why didn't Opie take the Colonel's bait initially?

_____

_____

A kiss on the hand—just the perfect touch.

"'We're no spring chickens anymore.' Well, maybe he isn't!"

"I'm not going to pay Doc Andrews five dollars just to tell me how old I am. And I'm not that old!"

Practiced deceivers know that emotions are powerful. They are quick to recognize the felt needs of others, using them to their own advantage.

The Colonel quickly sized up Aunt Bee. What did he see? How did he use it?

_____

_____

_____

Why was Aunt Bee so undiscerning about Colonel Harvey and his mission?

_____

_____

_____

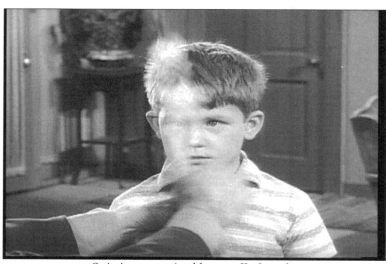

Opie is mesmerized by a puff of smoke.

Although initially uninterested, Opie also fell under the spell of the Colonel when he began to talk about Indians and smoke signals.

What does that tell you regarding the tactics of deception? Why are children particularly at risk?

_____

_____

_____

Andy normally likes people, but he remained very cool toward Colonel Harvey. Why do you think Andy did not see the Colonel the same way Aunt Bee did?

_____

_____

_____

If Andy had not intervened, how long do you think Aunt Bee might have continued to believe in Colonel Harvey?

_____

_____

Aunt Bee rips off a rousing ditty, with Opie's help.

2 TIMOTHY 1:13-14
Hold fast the pattern of sound words which you have heard from me, in faith and love which are in Christ Jesus. That good thing which was committed to you, keep by the Holy Spirit who dwells in us.
. (NKJV)

✝ ℙrinciple: **We should _____ ____ to the truth.**

Flattery is a sweet deception that makes us feel better at the moment, but leaves us worse off because it changes our focus from God to ourselves, from the absolute to the conditional.

What was the basic truth Aunt Bee failed to hold fast?
_____
_____
_____

If she had guarded this truth would she have been so vulnerable to a lie? Why or why not?
_____
_____
_____

At times, have you failed to hang on to the truth taught in God's Word?
❑ Yes ❑ No

If so, what got you back on track?
_____
_____
_____

"Oh, Colonel. You'll have to forgive the child. He's simply captivated by you. And I can't blame him."

"He ain't leaving right now. He's over at the house, addressing the Ladies Aide Church Committee right now."

"Oh, it's going to be a red-letter day in Mayberry if the whole Ladies Aide church committee gets crocked!"

Is deception more of a problem today than it was in the Mayberry era? Why or why not?

_____

_____

_____

Why do you think it is one of the devil's favorite weapons?

_____

_____

_____

Given what we have learned from Aunt Bee, how accessible to deception are you today?
(circle one)

Not at all ⟶ Extremely

1 2 3 4 5 6 7 8 9 10

Though a "magic elixir" may not tempt you, do you know what area in your life is most susceptible to deception?
❑ Yes ❑ No

_____

_____

_____

What could you do to strengthen your guard?

_____

_____

_____

Trusting Aunt Bee's discernment leads to an interesting meeting!

ROMANS 12:21
Do not be overcome by evil, but overcome evil with good. (NKJV)

✝ Principle: **We should _____ others snared by deception and _____ those who deceive.**

The quickest way to dispel a lie is to speak the truth in love. Andy did not want Aunt Bee to remain in deception. He showed godly wisdom and respect for Aunt Bee when he did not *confront* her perception of Colonel Harvey, but instead revealed who the Colonel really was.

Why is it important to respect the person we are trying to help?

_____
_____
_____

The Colonel tosses his hat to Andy, as he oils his way to the dining room.

Do you think you are prepared to speak the truth to others in love?
❑ Yes ❑ No

If not, what would you need to do to get ready?

_____
_____
_____

Do you know anyone who might need your help to break free from deception?
❑ Yes ❑ No ❑ Maybe

"The guy's a Grade A, double-barreled phoney!"

"I know. But Aunt Bee believes in him. If I run him out of town like this, she'll never forgive me. We'll have to prove it to her."

"That stuff of the Colonel's is supposed to purge the body and lift the spirit. Actually, what it does is give you a buzz. The Colonel calls it elixir. Other names are hooch, booze, happy water, old red eye. In other words, ladies, you got gassed!"

1 JOHN 2:24-26

Therefore let that abide in you which you heard from the beginning. If what you heard from the beginning abides in you, you also will abide in the Son and in the Father. And this is the promise that He has promised us--eternal life. These things I have written to you concerning those who try to deceive you. (NKJV)

✝ Principle: **We should seek the _____ for _____ judgment.**

Rather than giving ourselves to earthly fantasies, God calls us to focus on our eternal future with Him. As our heart grows toward God and His ways, our mind develops moral insight (Phil. 1:9-11).

Consider the following action points and plan to do at least one of them this week, with God's help.

I will resist deception by:
❑ Asking God to give me discernment about a specific temptation I face.
❑ Refusing to tell a lie that could get me out of trouble.

I will help others who are deceived by:
❑ Being available to someone in need.
❑ Sharing the Good News with someone who seems ready to hear it.
❑ Providing an example of the truth through my actions.

I will look to Jesus for the answers by:
❑ Spending an extra 15 minutes per day reading and studying God's Word.
❑ Asking God to show me where I am most susceptible to deception.

NOTES

NOTES

OTHER EZ LESSON PLANS

The EZ Lesson Plan was designed with the facilitator in mind. This new format gives you the flexibility as a teacher to use the video as the visual and then refer to the facilitator's guide for the questions….and even better, the answers. It is designed for a four-week study, communicated by our top authors and it is totally self contained. **Each EZ Lesson Plan requires the student's guides to be purchased separately as we have maintained a very low purchase price on the video resource.**

Please visit your local Christian bookstore to see the other titles we have available in the EZ Lesson Plan format. We have listed some of the titles and authors for your convenience:

EZ LESSON PLANS NOW AVAILABLE:

The 10 Commandments of Dating   Ben Young and Dr. Samuel Adams

Are you tired of pouring time, energy, and money into relationships that start off great and end with heartache? If so, you need The 10 Commandments of Dating to give you the hard -hitting, black-and-white, practical guid elines that will address your questions and frustrations about dating. This guide will help you keep your head in the search for the desire of your heart.
EZ Lesson Plan ISBN: 0-7852-9619-0   **Student's Guide ISBN: 0-7852-9621-2**

Extreme Evil: Kids Killing Kids   Bob Larson

Kids are killing kids in public schools! Kids are killing their parents! What is causing all of this evil in our younger generation? Do we need prayer back in the schools…or do we need God to start in the home? Bob Larson gets us to the root of these evils and brings us some of the answers we are looking for in this new video assisted program.
EZ Lesson Plan ISBN: 0-7852-9701-4   **Student's Guide ISBN: 0-7852-9702-2**

Life Is Tough, but God Is Faithful   Sheila Walsh

Sheila take s a look at eight crucial turning points that can help you rediscover God's love and forgiveness. Showing how the choices you make affect your life, she offers insights from the book of Job, from her own life, and from the lives of people whose simple but determined faith helped them become shining lights in a dark world.
EZ Lesson Plan ISBN: 0-7852-9618-2   **Student's Guide ISBN: 0-7852-9620-4**

Why I Believe   D. James Kennedy

In this video, Dr. D. James Kennedy offers intelligent, informed response s to frequently heard objections to the Christian faith. By dealing with topics such as the Bible, Creation, the Resurrection and the return of Christ, Why I Believe provides a solid foundation for Christians to clarify their own thinking while becoming more articulate in the defense of their faith.
EZ Lesson Plan ISBN: 0-7852-8770-9   **Student's Guide ISBN: 0-7852-8769-5**

The Lord's Prayer   **Jack Hayford**

Why do we say "Thy Kingdom come?" What does "Hallowed be Thy Name" mean? Do we really practice "Forgive us our debts as we forgive our debtors?" Pastor Jack Hayford walks you through verse by verse and then applies his great scripture to our personal lives. This study will put "meaning to the words" you have just been saying for years.

EZ Lesson Plan ISBN: 0-7852-9442-2   **Student's Guide ISBN: 0-7852-9609-3**

How To Pray   **Ronnie Floyd**

Whether you are a rookie in prayer or a seasoned prayer warrior, this video kit will meet you where you are and take you to another level in your prayer life. You may have been raised in a Christian home where prayer was a normal, daily exercise. You may have attended church all of your life, where the prayers of the people and the minister were as common as the hymns that still ring in your ears. Yet such experiences do not guarantee that you know how to pray. With simple, yet profound prose, Dr. Floyd declares, "prayer occurs when you depend on God, prayerlessness occurs when you depend on yourself."

EZ Lesson Plan ISBN: 0-8499-8790-3   **Student's Guide ISBN: 0-8499-8793-8**

Jesus and The Terminator   **Jack Hayford**

From the **E-Quake** Series comes the EZ Lesson Plan that is the focal point of the Book of Revelation. Pastor Hayford sets the stage for the fight against the Evil One when the end of time comes upon us. There is no greater force than that of Jesus and now viewers will see Him become triumphant again in this battle that is evident.

EZ Lesson Plan ISBN: 0-7852-9601-8   **Student's Guide ISBN: 0-7852-9658-1**

The Law of Process   **John C. Maxwell**

Leadership develops daily, not in a day. This law, taken from **The Twenty One Irrefutable Laws of Leadership** is the first of the series to be placed into an individual study. Take each opportunity as it comes along and find the answer in a way only strong leaders would do it….by processing it. John explains how and why "Champions don't become champions in the ring…they are merely recognized there."

EZ Lesson Plan ISBN: 0-7852-9671-9   **Student's Guide ISBN: 0-7852-9672-7**

Forgiveness   **John MacArthur**

In this three-session EZ Lesson Plan, noted biblical scholar John MacArthur provides an insightful look at forgiveness. MacArthur not only reminds us that we are called to grant forgiveness to those who sin against us, but he also teaches the importance of learning to accept the forgiveness of others.

EZ Lesson Plan ISBN: 0-8499-8808-X   **Student's Guide ISBN: 0-8499-8809-8**

EZ LESSON PLANS COMING SOON:

Healing Prayer   Reginald Cherry, M.D.

"Prayer is the divine key that unlocks God's pathway to healing in both the natural and supernatural realms of life." In Healing Prayer, he explores the connection between faith and healing, the Bible and medicine. Cherry blends the latest research, true stories, and biblical principles to show that spirit-directed prayers can bring healing for disease.

EZ Lesson Plan ISBN: 0-7852-9666-2   **Student's Guide ISBN: 0-7852-9667-0**

Andy Griffith - Volume Two Integrity   Systems Media, Inc.

For generations, stories have been used to teach universal truths. In keeping with this time-honored tradition, the new four volume Andy Griffith Bible Study Series has been developed, which uses the classic stories of Mayberry to illustrate biblical truths. In *Honesty*, the first volume of the series, learn from Andy, Opie, and the gang as they struggle with, and learn from, everyday life situations. In the second volume to be released in January the lesson uses the same characters but a new series of lessons on Integrrity.

EZ Lesson Plan ISBN: 0-8499-8815-2   **Student's Guide ISBN: 0-8499-8816-0**

Becoming A Woman of Grace   Cynthia Heald

This is a newly formatted product built around a message that only Cynthia Heald could deliver to us. Women have proven to be the stronger of the sexes in prayer, empathy and faith. Cynthia leads this women's group study on how a woman can become A Woman of Grace through prayer, obedience to God and other practices of their lives. This EZ Lesson Plan will bring the components of this publishing product to one, self-contained format ready to start small groups.

EZ Lesson Plan ISBN: 0-7852-9706-5   **Student's Guide ISBN: 0-7852-9707-3**

Created To Be God's Friend   Henry Blackaby

Henry Blackaby being born a man of God, living his life as a man of God, teaches us how all of us are created equal in being God's friend. No Christian need live without a keen sense of purpose, and no believer need give up on finding daily closeness with God.

EZ Lesson Plan ISBN: 0-7852-9718-9   **Student's Guide ISBN: 0-7852-9719-7**

Resurrection   Hank Hanegraaff

In this definitive work, popular Christian apologist Hank Hanegraaff offers a detailed defense of the Resurrection, the singularly most important event in history and the foundation upon which Christianity is built. Using the acronym F.E.A.T., the author examines the four distinctive, factual evidences of Christ's resurrection--Fatal torment, Empty tomb, Appearances, and Transformation--making the case for each in a memorable way that believers can readily use in their own defense of the faith.

EZ Lesson Plan ISBN: 0-8499-8798-9   **Student's Guide ISBN: 0-8499-8799-7**

The Murder of Jesus   **John MacArthur**

To many, the story of Christ's crucifixion has become so familiar that is has lost its ability to shock, outrage or stir any great emotion. In *The Murder of Jesus*, John MacArthur presents this pivotal moment in the life of Jesus in a way that forces the viewers to witness this event in all its power. The passion of Christ is examined chronoligically through the lens of the New Testament with special attention given to Jesus' words on the cross, the miracles that attended the crucifixion, and the significance of Christ's atoning work.

EZ Lesson Plan ISBN: 0-8499-8796-2   **Student's Guide ISBN: 0-8499-8797-0**

Fresh Brewed Life   **Nicole Johnson**

God is calling us to wake up, to shout an enthusiastic "Yes" to life, just as we say "Yes" to our first cup of coffee each morning. Nothing would please Him more than for us to live fresh-brewed lives steeped with His love, filling the world with the marvelous aroma of Christ. The EZ Lesson Plan will provide humor, vignettes, and in depth study to small groups all over on this topic.

EZ Lesson Plan ISBN: 0-7852-9723-5   **Student's Guide ISBN: 0-7852-9724-3**

The Law of Respect   **John C. Maxwell**

We are taught from our parents to respect others. Our business practices are to be ones of respecting others ideas, thoughts and mainly their motivations. We tend to get caught up in the daily routines, but if we do not respect those around us and the ones we work with, our success will be held at a low ebb. John Maxwell is a leader's leader.

EZ Lesson Plan ISBN: 0-7852-9756-1   **Student's Guide ISBN: 0-7852-9757-X**

The Ten Commandments   **Jack Hayford**

We are all taught the Ten Commandments early in our Christian walk. Dr. Jack Hayford now takes us one step farther and teaches us each of these commandments by a video-assisted method. Dr. Hayford teaches us to honor our fathers and our mothers by first teaching us to honor our Lord. All ten commandments will be taught over a four-session study. Studies with the comprehensive study material sold separately.

EZ Lesson Plan ISBN: 0-7852-9771-5   **Student's Guide ISBN: 0-7852-9772-3**

Fit To Be a Lady   **Kim Camp**

Kim Camp shows moms how to make it through the difficult years of parenting pre-adolescent daughters by nurturing their girls in the love and grace of God--the source of all self-worth and confidence. Camp examines such topics as peer influences, music and the media, sex and purity, and diet and exercise.

EZ Lesson Plan ISBN: 0-8499-8827-6   **Student's Guide ISBN: 0-8499-8828-4**